W9-CEJ-670

Great Disasters

Emma Hahn

J. WESTON
WALCH
PUBLISHER

Portland, Maine

1   2   3   4   5   6   7   8   9   10

ISBN 0-8251-2789-0

Copyright © 1996
J. Weston Walch, Publisher
P. O. Box 658 • Portland, Maine 04104-0658
Printed in the United States of America

Contents

Introduction

Disasters have occurred throughout the history of the world. Great loss of life and property often come from great disasters. Some we know about from records and stories. Others, more ancient, we only know from the shape of the earth. Its cracks, glaciers, rocks, rivers, and forests often give us clues to past disasters.

Some of the world's greatest disasters—such as tornadoes, earthquakes, and floods—have been caused by nature. Others—such as aircraft tragedies—have been caused by human inventions.

How we deal with disaster is more important than finding blame. People often come together to help one another in extraordinary ways during disasters. It is a good lesson in how people might work together better in their everyday lives.

Another thing to be learned from great disasters is whether we can prevent them in the future. Sometimes we can take steps to prevent them. But some natural disasters are totally out of people's control. So we can learn how to cope better with the disasters as they are happening, and we can learn how to rebuild later from their destruction.

All of the disasters in this book really happened.

Volcanic Eruptions: Mount Vesuvius and Krakatoa

AP/WIDE WORLD PHOTOS

Mount Vesuvius may be the most famous volcano in history. It is located on the Bay of Naples in the southwestern part of Italy. Before A.D. 79, generations of people had farmed the rich soil on the hillsides of Vesuvius. They never thought that they were living on an active volcano. Two great Roman cities, Pompeii and Herculaneum, were thriving cultural centers built on the slopes of Mount Vesuvius.

On August 24, A.D. 79, a huge cloud appeared over Vesuvius. A Roman named Pliny the Younger described the cloud as "an immense tree trunk projected into the air, and opened out with branches . . . sometimes white and sometimes mottled."

During the night, Pliny watched the volcano from the safety of an island. He wrote, "Above the mountain the night sky was often ripped by sudden bursts of fire, writhing snakelike and revealing sudden flashes larger than lightning."

On the mountain itself, citizens were jolted awake by a series of sharp earthquakes. This was their only warning before a gigantic explosion blew the top off 4000-foot Mount Vesuvius. Fiery ash shot out of the volcano. The citizens of Pompeii died of suffocation and poisonous gases. Their city was buried under 20 feet of ash and pumice. The people of Herculaneum were drowned as torrential rains turned the ash into a river of gray mud. An avalanche of mud hit the city like a giant bulldozer. It buried Herculaneum under 65 feet of volcanic debris in places. Over 20,000 lives were lost. Both Pompeii and Herculaneum remained buried for 1600 years.

1800 years later, on August 27, 1883, the biggest volcanic eruption in history shook the world. For centuries, **Krakatoa** had been just another lush, green island in the strait between Java and Sumatra in the East Indies. Sailors took little note of Krakatoa's volcanic mountain before May 1883. Then, the captain of a German sailing ship reported seeing a strange vapor cloud over the island. The cloud rose over six miles high, and the captain could hear explosions and flashes of lightning coming from the cloud. But after several days the cloud faded away. Everything seemed normal until August 27.

It was a clear, sunny Sunday morning. People were on their way to church. Suddenly, they were stopped in their tracks as a huge explosion blasted the region. Historians say the sound has never been equaled on earth. It was heard 1800 miles away in the Philippines, 1900 miles away in western Australia, and 2000 miles away in Ceylon and India. Four hours later the sound reached the island of Rodrigues, 3000 miles away in the Indian Ocean. Shock waves created by the sound traveled at least seven times around the world.

An enormous black cloud, shooting out hot ash and pumice, soared to a height of 17 miles above the crater of the volcano. The sky was darkened for 50 miles around the volcano. The island literally blew itself apart. But the worst destruction was yet to come.

The violence of the underwater explosion, combined with the enormous masses of falling material, created huge tsunamis.* Giant walls of water, some hundreds of feet tall, swept across the ocean. The huge waves traveled at speeds up to 350 miles per hour. By the time it hit the coast of Java, one wave was estimated to be about 125 feet tall; it was the size of a 12-story building. The water destroyed everything in its path. 295 villages were wiped out, and over 5000 ships were sunk. A large steamship was carried over a mile inland and dumped behind a hill. (It remains there today.) More than 36,000 people lost their lives.

In 1927 a new volcano began to grow from the floor of Krakatoa's crater. It has been named Anak Krakatoa (the "Child of Krakatoa"). It is now over 300 feet high. We may not have heard the last from this mighty giant Krakatoa.

---

* *tsunami* (soo • na̤‥′ • mē) tidal wave

Activities

Remembering the Facts

Decide whether each of the following statements about the story is true or false. Write **True** or **False** next to each sentence.

1. Mount Vesuvius is located on the Italian island of Sicily.

2. Mount Vesuvius erupted in 79 B.C.

3. Everyone in Herculaneum drowned in rivers of hot lava.

4. Krakatoa is situated in the West Indies.

5. Pliny was the name of the Roman who wrote about the eruption of Mount Vesuvius.

6. It's impossible to farm the land around a volcano.

7. When Krakatoa erupted in 1923, an entire island blew itself apart.

8. People could hear the explosions from Krakatoa as far away as Australia.

9. People had no warning about Krakatoa's eruption in 1883.

10. Other Roman citizens quickly uncovered Pompeii and Herculaneum, but they found no survivors.

Understanding the Story

Write a short paragraph to answer one of the following questions.

1. A person who studies volcanoes is a **vulcanologist**. As a vulcanologist, what would be one of the first things you'd want to know about a volcano in your region? Why?

2. You have been warned that a tsunami is about to strike. Can you think of ways to protect yourself and your community?

Vocabulary

Write a sentence using each of these words from the stories about Mount Vesuvius and Krakatoa.

- eruption

- thriving

- cultural

- citizens

- suffocation

- torrential

- pumice

- strait

- vapor

- crater

Earthquake:
San Francisco, 1906

AP/WIDE WORLD PHOTOS

The greatest fracture in the earth's surface—called the San Andreas Fault—is located in California. It is a constant threat to the people there. And on April 18, 1906, at 5:12 A.M., the earth shifted vertically as much as 21 feet—for nearly 250 miles—along this dangerous fault line.

The slippage in the San Andreas Fault shook an area about 250 miles long, 40 miles inland, and unknown distances out to sea. Unfortunately, the city of San Francisco was right over the epicenter of this massive earthquake.

San Franciscans were proud of the ways their city had developed from a gold rush town in 1849 to a cultural and business center in 1906. The night before the fateful earthquake, many of its 450,000 residents had celebrated. The great international opera star Enrico Caruso had come to perform in their Opera House.

Ironically, Caruso was delighted to be in San Francisco, because the timing kept him away from an eruption of Mount Vesuvius, in Naples, Italy. He went to sleep feeling grateful that God had spared him—only to be thrown on the floor by the earthquake in San Francisco the next morning. Caruso was terrified as his bed rocked about his room like a storm-tossed ship. Pictures fell off the walls, the ceiling collapsed, and bureau drawers were scattered about the room.

Caruso ran out in the street; glass and bricks rained down on him. He saw trolley tracks twisted and uprooted. Huge cracks opened in the streets, exposing wild tangles of wires. Some of the wires were sparking. Water shot out of broken mains from other cracks; he could smell gas leaking.

Within 10 minutes hot coals from fallen stoves, live wires touching wood, and escaping gas lit by flames started fires all over the city. It did not take long for all the small fires to merge into one huge conflagration. Neighborhoods were consumed by flames. Smoke could be seen a hundred miles out to sea. The heat was so intense that houses across the street from those on fire ignited by spontaneous combustion.

Dennis Sullivan, San Francisco's fire chief, was one of the first to die. When the earthquake awakened him, he ran in the dark to the door of the next room, opened it, and fell three stories. He died shortly after without ever becoming conscious.

Sullivan's firefighters had little hope of putting out the fires. The underground water mains had broken during the quake. The only water was what they could pump up from the bay. Their equipment could not pump that water much beyond the docks. However, the firefighters saved much of the wharf area. Ferryboats could land and carry passengers safely out of the city. Caruso was one of the first to escape this way. But the docks soon became crowded. People frantically pushed, struggled, and tried to bribe their way onto boats. Over 55,000 people escaped across the bay to Oakland.

Finally, the only way to stop the fire from destroying the entire city was to create a firebreak. One of the widest streets in the city (125 feet wide) was Van Ness Avenue. People were told to leave all the remaining houses on this avenue. Then soldiers aimed a row of cannons at them. They knocked down 16 blocks, or 1 mile, of some of the finest houses in San Francisco. It worked. The fire did not cross the break. Then the wind shifted and a light rain began to fall.

On April 21, three days after the earthquake, the last fire in San Francisco was put out. When the smoke cleared, 4.7 miles in the heart of the city had been destroyed. More then 28,000 buildings were gutted. Over 500 people were known dead. Another 350 were missing and never found. And hundreds more were seriously injured.

But the people loved this city, even if it did sit on one of the biggest fault lines in the world. By the end of 1907 much of the rubble had been carried away. Three years after the great earthquake, 20,000 new homes had been built. The city was well on its way to recovery—at least, until the next earthquake!

Activities

Remembering the Facts

Decide whether each of the following statements about the story is true or false. Write **True** or **False** next to each sentence.

1. The city of San Francisco is situated right over the San Andreas Fault Line.

2. In the 1906 earthquake, the earth shifted more than 21 feet along a 300-mile stretch of the fault line.

3. The name of the famous opera star visiting San Francisco was Mario Lanza.

4. The chief of the San Francisco Fire Department was one of the first people killed in the quake.

5. There was plenty of water to fight the fires raging throughout the city.

6. Many people escaped the conflagration by boarding ferries that carried them across the bay to Oakland.

7. Van Ness Avenue was one of the narrowest streets in San Francisco.

8. The city burned for three days before the last fire was extinguished.

9. More than 300 people were killed in the fire.

10. The people began to rebuild their city almost immediately after the fire.

Understanding the Story

Write a short paragraph explaining what you might do in one of the following circumstances.

1. Imagine that you and your brother and sister are waiting to board a ferry to escape the fire. The captain says, "Sorry. We have room for only two more people." What will you do?

2. If you woke up at night and found your house on fire, how would you escape?

Vocabulary

Write a sentence using each of these words or phrases from the story.

- vertically

- fracture

- fault line

- epicenter

- opera

- ironically

- trolley

- conflagration

- spontaneous combustion

- gutted

The Molasses Flood

AP/WIDE WORLD PHOTOS

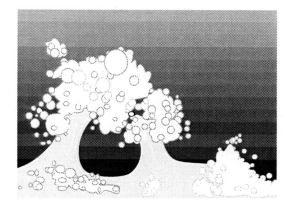

On January 15, 1919, a steel tank that was 50 feet tall and 90 feet across split open. More than 2 million tons of molasses poured out over unsuspecting citizens of Boston, Massachusetts.

It was 43 degrees Fahrenheit—unusually warm for mid-January. Workers in the downtown Boston freight yard next to the towering molasses tank had removed their heavy winter coats to enjoy the weather. They had loaded four freight cars. A fifth was only half full when the workers decided to take their lunch break.

Sitting in the noon sun, they watched a woman from the neighborhood hang her blankets out on a line. They also saw a little blond-haired girl, Maria Di Stasio, collecting firewood under the freight cars as they talked about the unusual warm spell.

Their supervisor called out to the men, asking them to finish loading the last freight car. Just then, they heard a deep rumble. The earth shook under their feet. There was a ripping, tearing sound as bolts snapped out of the sides of the molasses tank. It seemed as if steel bullets were whizzing over the workers' heads as the bolts flew through the air. The people then heard a huge roar as the bottom of the tank split open. A giant, 30-foot-high wall of yellow-foaming molasses burst across the street. This tidal wave of molasses crushed everything in its path.

The four loaded freight cars were washed like matchsticks down the track. The fifth, half-empty one, was swept up on the molasses wave. It crashed through the iron wall of the freight terminal. Molasses poured into the freight terminal, sweeping freight clerks right off their feet. They tried to swim in the muck, but the sticky stuff pulled them down and drowned them. Workers caught in the cellar of the terminal tried to dash up the stairs to escape. But they slipped and disappeared in the sticky yellow river.

Men, women, children, and animals caught by the wave were drowned. The wave ripped away the supports under some elevated tracks—just seconds after a train had safely passed.

It even toppled the fire station.

When the first wave passed, molasses—three feet deep in places—clogged the streets.

The neighbor woman's body was found in a tangle of molasses-soaked blankets.

A fireman spotted Maria Di Stasio's blond curls floating on top of the molasses. He plunged his arms into the sticky mess and pulled up her body. She was still clutching small sticks of firewood.

Twenty-one people were killed in all.

The next day, firefighters tried to hose the molasses off the buildings and wreckage with saltwater. But the water made the molasses foam up in yellow suds.

Cleaning up the gooey mess took weeks. Years later, people could still detect the smell of molasses in some crannies where the sticky flood had forced its way.

The tank owners paid nearly a million dollars in property damages—a fortune at that time. A court ruled that the molasses tank was not strong enough to hold the 2,500,000 gallons of molasses the owners had claimed it could.

Activities

Remembering the Facts

Complete the following statements with facts found in this story.

1. The molasses flood happened on one of the warmest days in _____.

2. The tank was made of wood held together with _____ bolts.

3. When the tank split open, over _____ gallons of molasses gushed into the street.

4. _____ freight cars were washed away in the flood.

5. The tank towered 58 feet in the air and measured _____ feet across.

6. The flood tore away the supports under an elevated _____ track.

7. When the tank burst, its steel bolts shot through the air like _____.

8. Nearly _____ dozen people were killed in this disaster.

9. The owners of the tank had to pay over _____ dollars in property damages.

10. Firefighters tried using _____ water in their hoses to clean up the molasses.

Understanding the Story

Write a short paragraph to answer one of the following questions.

1. How would you have checked the tank to make certain it could hold the molasses, even on warm days?

2. How well do you know the people in your neighborhood? Would you know who was missing if this kind of disaster struck?

Vocabulary

Write a sentence using each of the following words from the story.

- molasses

- unsuspecting

- freight

- supervisor

- terminal

- clerks

- elevated

- wreckage

- detect

- crannies

Killer Splash

ILLUSTRATION BY LOIS LEONARD STOCK

The tallest wave ever recorded in human history occurred on July 9, 1958, in Alaska. Lituya Bay is a fjordlike, T-shaped inlet on the southern coast of Alaska, where the Fairweather Range of the Saint Elias Mountains meets the sea. Three glaciers feed into this bay. It is one of the most beautiful—and one of the most dangerous—bodies of water on earth.

A French explorer named François de La Perouse sailed into the inlet in 1786. He described Lituya Bay as "perhaps the most extraordinary place in the world . . . a basin of water whose depth could not be fathomed, bordered by peaked mountains of an excessive height, covered with snow . . . . I never saw a breath of air ruffle the surface of this water; it is never troubled but by the fall of enormous pieces of ice."

For the most part, the inlet was left to fish, birds, and seals until the middle of the twentieth century. On July 9, 1958, two fishing boats—the *Edrie* and the *Badger*—were anchored just outside the bay. A third boat, the *Sunmore*, was steaming through the inlet. Suddenly, a massive earthquake struck. It caused a huge slab (90 million tons) of rock and ice to fall from the face of the glacier. The giant slab fell nearly half a mile down into the water from the northeast side of the bay.

The mammoth chunk of glacier created a splash that sent a solid sheet of water racing across the bay at 130 miles per hour. The wave surged 1740 feet (twice the height of the Eiffel Tower) over the mountain on the opposite shore. It stripped four square miles of forest down to bare rock.

The *Sunmore* and all her crew disappeared without a trace. The *Edrie* capsized and sank. The men on board the *Badger*, however, had the ride of their lives.

They were paralyzed with fear when they saw the giant wave racing toward their boat. The boat was riding directly toward the wave—actually, the only position in which the boat stood a chance. The horrified men watched as the roaring wave engulfed them and their boat. It carried their boat straight upward. When the boat's hull (bottom) was nearly vertical to the horizon, it carved its way through the crest of the wave.

Sailing on the crest of the giant wave, the terrified crew looked down on the tops of tall trees at least 80 feet below them. Then it careened down the back side of the wave at breakneck speed. The craft lurched sickeningly as the surge flattened beneath them. No one could believe they had remained afloat.

The wave safely carried the *Badger* over Point LaChausse, at the mouth of the bay. The boat dropped—with almost no damage—into the ocean outside the inlet.

Activities

Remembering the Facts

Complete the following statements with facts from this story.

1. Lituya Bay is a _____ inlet in Alaska.

2. _____ glaciers feed into the bay.

3. One of the mountain ranges bordering the inlet is
    _____.

4. The "Killer Splash" happened in 19____.

5. All the crew on board the _____ survived.

6. The splash was created when a huge slab of
    _____ fell over half a mile down into the bay.

7. The fishing boat _____ capsized and sank.

8. The terrified crew could look down at trees _____ feet
    below them as they flew over the top of the splash.

9. The splash raced across the inlet at _____ miles per hour.

10. The force of the water stripped _____ square miles of forest down to bare rock.

Understanding the Story

Write a short paragraph explaining how you might react to one of the following situations.

1. Have you ever been seasick? What would you do to keep calm and steady if you saw a giant wave racing toward your boat?

2. If you saw a beautiful spot like Lituya Bay, and noticed that it was not crawling with tourist boats, would you wonder why? What would you want to know about this body of water before you sailed into it? How would you find out?

Vocabulary

Write a sentence using each of the following words from this story.

- fjordlike

- inlet

- glaciers

- fathomed

- anchored

- mammoth

- capsized

- crest

- careened

- lurched

The *Hindenburg*

AP/WIDE WORLD PHOTOS

On May 3, 1937, the German dirigible *Hindenburg* took off from Frankfurt, Germany. The *Hindenburg* was a special kind of dirigible: It was a zeppelin. Zeppelins are built with light, rigid metal frames that hold huge bags of lighter-than-air gas. The frame and bags are covered with an outside "skin." The gas lifts the zeppelins off the ground, and the crew uses propellers and rudders to guide and steer the ships.

The *Hindenburg* was the largest airship ever built. At 972 feet long, it was larger than three football fields. Linen fabric covered its metal framework, inside of which were 16 huge gas bags. The bags were filled with 7,300,000 cubic feet of hydrogen. The bags had to be inspected often for leaks, because a mixture of hydrogen and oxygen can burn with explosive force.

The bags could have been filled with helium, which does not burn, but the United States was the major producer of this lightweight gas in the 1930's. Their supply was so limited they did not sell it to any other countries. Also, some people did not want to sell it to the Germans, for fear they might use it in warfare.

The *Hindenburg* was powered by four 16-cylinder Daimler Benz diesel engines. Each engine produced 1100 horsepower to push the ship through the air at a speed of 84 miles per hour. Diesel engines were used because diesel fuel was safer than gasoline.

Known as the "Queen of the Air," the dirigible was heading for Lakehurst, New Jersey—3895 miles across Europe and the Atlantic Ocean. The *Hindenburg* had made ten earlier trips to the United States, but this was its first 1937 voyage. Radio announcers and reporters were on hand to report as the giant airship landed at Lakehurst.

Ninety-seven passengers, of five different nationalities, were on board. One was an acrobat named Joseph Spah. He had been performing in circuses all over Europe, and his wife and three children anxiously awaited his return in the United States.

The seventy-two-hour trip from Frankfurt to Lakehurst went smoothly. As the ship flew over New York City, people leaned out of windows to look. Photographers stood on top of the Empire State Building to get pictures. People said the ship looked like a great feather sliding through the air.

But just as it approached the landing field in New Jersey, the *Hindenburg* met a thunderstorm. The captain flew back out to sea to let the storm pass. Three hours later, when the Naval Air Station said the weather was better, the captain returned to the field. When the ship was 200 feet above the mooring, the crew began to drop the landing ropes. They first threw ropes from the nose of the ship to the ground crew waiting below.

Then, as the crew prepared to drop landing ropes from the rear of the airship, they heard a strange pop. At the same moment, a reporter spotted a burst of flame at the rear of the ship. Within seconds, the hydrogen exploded. One by one, each of the four tanks blew up. People 15 miles away could hear the explosions.

Covered in flames, the ship started sinking to the ground. The crew and passengers were trapped inside.

Then, 35 feet above the ground, a man jumped out of the burning airship. He turned a somer-sault as he hit the ground, then ran as the flaming wreckage plunged to the earth. His name was Joseph Spah; he was one of the few survivors of this terrible disaster.

It only took 32 seconds for the *Hindenburg* to fall and 35 of its passengers and crew to die.

No one ever found out what started the fire. Some people thought it might be sabotage. There had been rumors that the airship would be blown up if it tried to land in the United States. The flight had never been fully booked. Even when the Germans offered to give people free seats, many said no. And after the tragic accident, Hermann Goering, Chief of the Nazi air force, ordered the surviving officers and crew of the *Hindenburg* to "stop trying to find an explanation."

This was the last time passengers were ever carried on a dirigible.

Activities

Remembering the Facts

Decide whether each of the following statements about this air tragedy is true or false. Write **True** or **False** next to each sentence.

1. The *Hindenburg* was built in Germany.

2. Thirty-seven passengers from ten different countries were on board this fatal flight.

3. The 3895 mile trip from Frankfurt, Germany, took three days.

4. Radio and TV newscasters were on hand to greet the "Queen of the Air" when she landed.

5. The 16 hydrogen-filled air bags had to be inspected regularly for leaks.

6. The giant zeppelin exploded without warning.

7. A circus clown who jumped 30 feet from the flaming wreck was one of the few survivors.

8. The *Hindenburg* was longer than the combined length of three football fields.

9. The landing at Lakehurst was temporarily delayed because of a blinding snowstorm.

10. No one knows what really caused this great air tragedy.

Understanding the Story

Write a short paragraph following one of the following suggestions.

1. Pretend you are a reporter. Describe how the magnificent *Hindenburg* looked gliding through the air before the explosion.

2. Describe how you think it would feel to fly over tall buildings in such an airship. (Include details like sound, temperature, and how the people on the ground look from the air.)

Vocabulary

Write a sentence using each of the following words from this story.

- dirigible

- propellers

- rudders

- linen

- hydrogen

- helium

- diesel

- horsepower

- acrobat

- sabotage

The Tri-State Tornado

AP/WIDE WORLD PHOTOS

The 1925 Tri-State Tornado was the most destructive single tornado in American history. It began at about 1:00 P.M. in Missouri. In a little over three hours it had blasted a 219-mile path of death and destruction across Missouri, Illinois, and Indiana.

The storm's funnel cloud varied in width between a half-mile and a mile. It traveled at speeds from 57 to 68 miles per hour. In three ways (distance covered, size, and speed), this tornado was truly much bigger than average.

Tornadoes—often called twisters—are some of the most destructive storms on earth. A tornado is a giant funnel-shaped "finger" of cyclonic winds. Wind speeds can reach several hundred miles per hour, rushing down to the earth from dark cumulonimbus clouds.

Tornadoes can wreak havoc in three ways: (1) the powerful winds on the edges of the funnel can blow down trees and buildings; (2) the extreme drop in air pressure can cause sealed buildings to explode; (3) the strong updraft winds inside the funnel can pick up houses, cars, and many other heavy objects—sometimes carrying these things for miles before letting them crash back to the ground.

The tornado may only touch the ground for a few minutes, but it destroys everything in its path. The path itself can be as narrow as 3 yards or as wide as 2 miles.

In 1925, the Tri-State Tornado badly damaged 30 towns. It totally demolished over 6 towns like Griffin, Indiana. The Tri-State Tornado also killed 689 people, injured over 13,000 others, and left over $18 million worth of property damage.

Annapolis, Missouri, was the first town hit by the tornado. The town lost all but three of its buildings as the storm whirled down its main street. One person had a lucky escape. He was working in the bay window of his office. When the storm hit, it caused most of the building around him to collapse. But somehow, the pillars supporting his window were left standing. He escaped unhurt.

Others weren't nearly as lucky. When the storm hit Murphysboro, it crumpled buildings, tossed houses into the air, snapped telephone poles, and uprooted trees. People were crushed under falling buildings, killed by flying debris, or picked up by the twister—which violently hurled them to their deaths.

Several freak accidents occurred. In one house, the kitchen walls and roof were blown away, but the dishes on the table were not touched. Outside the house, the raging winds drove a two-by-four board through the center of a tree trunk.

Four miners coming home from work were sucked out of their car. Then they were gently set down beside the road, but their car was smashed to bits. The debris was scattered down the road for miles.

Many people in DeSoto, Illinois, were blown into fields miles away from their homes. And timbers from their homes were found over 15 miles away.

A railroad engineer raced against death when the tornado funnel hit his train. It tore the cab of his engine off. But the engineer held on and gunned his engine right through the maelstrom.

A pair of pants with $95 in the pocket was found 39 miles away from its bare-bottomed owner.

The people in the path of the Tri-State Tornado had no warning before it struck. Today, most towns have tornado warning systems. When you hear the alarm, it's best to take shelter in your cellar, or under a table or bed if you don't have a cellar. If you are caught in the open, lie flat on the ground in a ditch, if possible.

Activities

Remembering the Facts

Complete the following sentences with facts from the story.

1. The Tri-State Tornado did great damage in three states: Missouri, Illinois, and _____.

2. A tornado's wind can pick up heavy objects like _____ and drop them miles away.

3. Tornadoes can do millions of dollars of damage in just a few _____.

4. A man's pants were ripped off and blown 39 miles away without losing any of the $_____ in a pocket.

5. A tornado looks like a giant _____-shaped "finger" of cyclonic winds.

6. The Tri-State Tornado's funnel cloud varied in width between _____ and _____.

7. The extreme drop in _____ accompanying
    a tornado can cause sealed houses to explode.

8. The first town hit by the Tri-State Tornado was
    _____, Missouri.

9. This tornado was so powerful it drove a 2 × 4 board
    through the center of a _____.

10. Outside, one of the safest ways to protect yourself
    during a tornado is to lie down in a _____.

Understanding the Story

Write a short paragraph explaining what you might
do in one of these emergencies.

1. You and your little brother are home alone when you
    hear the tornado warning siren.

2. Would you rather be indoors or out if you saw a
    tornado heading toward you?

Vocabulary

Write a sentence using each of the following words from the story.

- funnel

- cyclonic

- cumulonimbus

- wreak

- havoc

- air pressure

- updraft

- pillars

- debris

- maelstrom

The Johnstown Flood

AP/WIDE WORLD PHOTOS

April and May of 1880 were bitterly cold and wet months in western Pennsylvania. Seventy-five miles east of Pittsburgh, the city of Johnstown got over 40 inches of rain and snow. A heavy, steady rain swelled local rivers to the point of overflowing their banks. Johnstown sat at the bottom of a gorge 16 miles southeast of, and 400 feet below, the South Fork Dam.

The South Fork Dam, built in 1862, was a huge barricade made of earth—1000 feet long, 90 feet thick, and 120 feet high. It was the largest dam of its kind in the world. Behind the dam was a private, manmade lake called Lake Conemaugh. This largest manmade lake in the United States was owned by such wealthy business-men as Andrew Mellon, Henry Frick, Philander Knox, and Andrew Carnegie. They stocked the lake with bass and pickerel for their elite South Fork Fishing and Hunting Club.

Johnstown had a population of about 30,000 in 1889. Many of these people worked for the steel mill. They lived in rows of tenements. Every spring they heard that the dam was weak and might not hold back the millions of tons of water in the $3\frac{1}{2}$-mile-long lake behind it. But no one paid any attention to the warnings. The citizens did not know that the club had placed grates over the drains and spillways to protect their stock of fish in the lake. With the drains not working, there was no way to relieve the pressure against the earthen dam from the 20 million tons of water held in the lake.

At 3:00 P.M. on May 31, water started pouring over the top of the dam. Some men frantically tried to free the drains, but it was hopeless. They heard strange rumblings from deep within the dam. Soon the water pouring over the top cut a *V* in the dam. Then, at 3:15, the dam exploded out into the valley. Twenty million tons of water roared down the gorge in a 50-foot-high wall of water.

Three small towns between the dam and Johnstown were completely destroyed. No one could be warned, because telegraph lines had come down in the storm the night before. The thundering wall of water uprooted trees and tore houses off their foundations. Train cars, and 33 engines weighing 75 tons each, were caught up in the 60-mile-per-hour torrent. This mountain of debris hit Johnstown like a battering ram. The city was quickly destroyed. It happened so fast that the people never stood a chance. They drowned or were crushed by the debris.

The only thing strong enough to stop the floodwater was the Stone Bridge. It had been built over the Conemaugh River by the Pennsylvania Railroad. The bridge was 50 feet wide on top (to carry 4 train tracks), 32 feet in height, and had seven 60-foot stone arches. It was built on a diagonal across the river. This helped save the bridge from collapse when the huge mass of debris hit it.

Horribly, though, the arches of the bridge soon became clogged with debris. The wreckage piled up, creating a terrible half-human, half-nonhuman dam. Hundreds of people were trapped in the pileup. Then it caught fire. Within minutes it became an inferno.

A few people managed to escape. One woman was held with her foot in the frozen grip of a dead man. A rescue worker had to cut off the man's arm to set her free. Another man cut off his own arm to get away from the flames.

The fire burned for days without seeming to make the pile of wreckage smaller. Finally a professional dynamiter was called in. But it still took over a week of explosions to move the mass.

Over 2200 people lost their lives in the Johnstown flood—300 of them at Stone Bridge. Hundreds of bodies never identified lie in unmarked graves. Property damage was about $18,000,000—a huge sum for that time.

Still, there were some amazing escapes. One 5-month-old baby rode the flood waters on the floor of a house 75 miles to Pittsburgh—where rescuers picked him up unharmed!

Activities

Remembering the Facts

Complete the following sentences with facts from the story.

1. The South Fork Dam was made of _____.

2. Many Johnstown citizens worked in _____.

3. Two businessmen who helped establish the
   South Fork Fishing and Hunting Club were
   _____ and _____.

4. The wall of water that roared down the gorge was
   _____ feet high.

5. The club had placed grates over the dam drains to

   _____.

6. The dam broke in the shape of a _____.

7. Johnstown was situated _____ miles from the dam.

8. In between the dam and Johnstown there were

    _____ other towns.

9. A baby survived by riding on _____
    to Pittsburgh.

10. The South Fork Dam was the _____ of its
    kind in the world.

Understanding the Story

Write a short paragraph in response to one of the
following questions.

1. How might someone have checked to make sure the
    dam was strong?

2. What are some of the other dangers *besides* the huge
    rush of water caused by flooding?

Vocabulary

Write a sentence using each of the following words from this flood story.

- gorge

- stocked

- elite

- tenements

- spillways

- telegraph

- torrent

- debris

- battering ram

- diagonal

Bhopal Gas Leak

AP/WIDE WORLD PHOTOS

December 3, 1984: The air grew cool and the streets quieted. Evening fell on Jayaprakash Nagar, a crowded slum in the city of Bhopal, India. The slum had been built just across the street from a huge Union Carbide chemical plant. Inside the small houses—some no more than huts—parents put their children to bed. Outside, cows, dogs, and goats that roamed freely settled down for the night. A gentle breeze picked up.

The pesticides made at the chemical plant were especially strong. It was part of a 1980's government program to "green" India, making it better for farming. One product from the plant could be used on 100 different crops against 180 different kinds of insects. It could kill within 24 hours. The people would soon find that this chemical had an equally devastating effect on humans.

Sometime in the night, a leak formed in an underground storage tank. All safety systems failed. Methyl isocyanate (a chemical used to make pesticides) rushed out of the tank. The chemical's deadly fumes were carried by the night breeze into the streets and houses of Jayaprakash Nagar. The fumes also entered a neighboring slum, Kali Parade, and the city of Bhopal.

Unfortunately, the weather was cool and misty. This allowed a cloud containing about 5 tons of deadly gas to settle over a 25-square-mile section of Bhopal. The effects were immediate. Some people died in their sleep as the gas filled the air passages in their lungs. Eyewitnesses reported thousands of other people running from their homes, screaming in pain as the gas burned their lungs and eyes. They could not breathe; red foam was frothing from their mouths.

But it wasn't just people who died. Thousands of animals were also killed by the lethal gas. Their carcasses littered the streets—attracting many starving dogs, vultures, and rats. People could not bury the dead fast enough. They had to burn the bodies—animal and human—to prevent a disease epidemic.

All of the poison gas disappeared in three days. But its effects would be felt for years. More than 6000 people died and over 70,000 were injured. Survivors have suffered from blindness; sterility; lung, kidney, and liver damage; and mental illness.

People have asked why Union Carbide ever built this chemical plant in such a populated area. (The city of Bhopal had over 800,000 inhabitants.) In fact, however, the plant had been built in a rather isolated area. The problem was that jobs created by building the plant attracted thousands of workers. Most of these people were very poor, so they built shelters as close to the plant as possible. Sadly, they had come to work at the plant to improve the quality of their lives.

Activities

Remembering the Facts

Decide whether each of the following statements about the story is true or false. Write **True** or **False** next to each sentence.

1. The accident occurred in June 1984.

2. Jayaprakash Nagar is a slum on the outskirts of the city of Bhopal.

3. The population of Bhopal at the time of the accident was 8,000,000.

4. The chemical plant involved was owned by Exxon.

5. It was the middle of the afternoon when the leak occurred.

6. Lethal gas escaped from an underground storage tank.

7. Methyl isocyanate is a chemical used in making pesticides.

8. More than 6000 people died and over 70,000 were injured in this industrial accident.

9. All the safety systems failed in this accident.

10. Fortunately, brisk winds blew the cloud of poison gas away from the city within minutes.

Understanding the Story

Write a short paragraph describing your reaction to one of the following questions.

1. Why did so many people live so close to a possibly dangerous factory?

2. Why do people use pesticides? Do you think they are usually helpful or harmful?

Vocabulary

- slum

- pesticides

- devastating

- frothing

- lethal

- carcasses

- epidemic

- sterility

- inhabitants

- isolated

Barnum Circus Tent Fire

AP/WIDE WORLD PHOTOS

It was July 6, 1944. The circus had just arrived in Hartford, Connecticut, from Providence, Rhode Island. It was a blistering hot day—so hot that Emmett Kelly, a famous clown, had trouble getting his putty nose to stick.

Despite the heat, 7000 people crowded into the giant bigtop of the Ringling Brothers Barnum and Bailey Circus. They couldn't wait to see the performers and the wild animals. There were a thousand animals in all—including 40 lions, 30 tigers, 30 leopards, 20 bears, 40 elephants, and a huge gorilla.

The bigtop tent, 520 feet long, was covered by the largest piece of canvas in the world. It weighed over 19 tons. The canvas had recently been sprayed with paraffin mixed with gasoline. This was done to make the bigtop more waterproof. No one seemed to know that this made the canvas very, very flammable.

Inside, high rows of bleachers lined the sides of the tent. Folding chairs had been set up at ringside for special guests.

The lions had just completed their act. The Flying Wallendas were climbing up the poles to get ready for their high-wire performance.

The bandleader suddenly noticed a small spot of flame over the main entrance. He ordered the band to play "Stars and Stripes Forever." All circus people know this song is an alarm—their warning that disaster is about to strike.

Immediately the Wallendas started down from their high wire. The clowns and crew tried to move the audience outside the tent. People couldn't understand why they were being marched out. Then a sudden breeze whipped the spot of fire into a sheet of flame. When they saw flames shooting across the roof of the tent, the people panicked. They started trampling one another in their frantic efforts to get out.

Some people climbed up the bleachers and jumped off the top to safety. Mothers tossed children from the bleacher tops, hoping that someone below would catch them. To go back into the tent meant sure death.

Others were not so lucky. The fire burned through the support poles. Then the flaming canvas—covered with gas and paraffin—fell. The people inside were engulfed in fire.

Fire engines arrived quickly, but the fire spread too fast. In minutes, 168 people (one third of them children) were killed. Another 500 were injured. The smoke was so thick that firefighters could not see whether people were still inside the tent.

Luckily, most of the animals were safe in their cages outside the bigtop.

It took years for Barnum and Bailey to pay millions of dollars in death claims. Because of this tragedy, very few circuses perform under a canvas bigtop today.

Only one victim was never identified. She had been smothered by the smoke. There were no burns or any other marks on her body. Still, no one came to claim her. The little blond, blue-eyed girl, about nine years old, became "Little Miss 1565" (from the number given her by police). The Hartford Fire Department buried her with a simple tombstone that says "Little Miss 1565." Every year on July 6 (the day of the Barnum circus fire), a firefighter, police officer, or caring citizen comes to place a small wreath on the little girl's grave.

Activities

Remembering the Facts

Choose words from this tragic fire story to complete each of the following statements.

1. The circus had just arrived in Hartford, Connecticut, from _____.

2. _____, the famous clown, had trouble getting his putty nose to stay on.

3. The bigtop canvas was the _____ in the world.

4. The fire was first spotted by _____.

5. The Flying Wallendas' act followed the

_____.

6. To escape, some people climbed up the bleachers and

_____.

7. As an alarm, the band began to play

   _____.

8. The circus tent was _____ feet long.

9. The giant bigtop was made of a single piece of

   _____.

10. The bigtop had been waterproofed with a combination of paraffin and _____.

Understanding the Story

Write a short paragraph to answer one of the following questions.

1. What would you do if you could be anything you wanted in the circus?

2. How would you have tried to escape from this blazing inferno?

Vocabulary

Write a sentence using each of the following words from this story.

- blistering

- putty

- canvas

- paraffin

- flammable

- ringside

- engulfed

- smothered

- identified

- tombstone

The Blizzard of '88

AP/WIDE WORLD PHOTOS

"Light snow, then clearing" was the weather forecast for March 12, 1888, in New York City.

In 1888, weather predictions were not as accurate as they can be today. There were no weather satellites or radar then. Forecasts were based on local weather, or on messages telegraphed from one part of the country to another.

Two days before, on March 10, 1888, temperatures were in the fifties in New York City. People were excited about having an early spring. They had no idea that a mass of frigid air was moving down from Canada at great speed. Nor did they know that a warm, wet air mass in the South was beginning to move north. And they certainly had no way of knowing that these two very different air masses would soon meet over New York City.

At this time the population of New York City was about 1,500,000 people. Even in the best weather, it was the biggest and most crowded city in the United States. A blinding snowstorm could be a disaster. But that's just what happened on March 12. When the icy Canadian air—with swirling snow and gale-force winds—met up with the windy, rainy tropical storm, a "Great White Hurricane" was born.

On March 11, a light rain began to fall. People went to sleep thinking the rain would taper off during the night. But they were stunned to wake up to a huge blizzard the next morning. Before noon, the snow was 2 feet deep with drifts up to 5 feet. Within hours, the depth rose to 5 feet deep with drifts up to 18 feet. Winds swept across the city at 84 miles per hour; the temperature crashed to 4 degrees below zero. The city and surrounding towns came to a stop. People who had been on their way to work were stranded.

New York City's elevated trains stopped in their tracks. About 15,000 people were stuck high above the streets, in crowded and unheated cars. A few clever people ran home for ladders. Then they charged the stranded folks $2 each to climb down out of the trains into the snow-clogged streets below.

Those workers who did make it to their offices often found them empty. And, now that the storm was so intense, it was almost impossible to get back home. Some who tried were frozen before they could reach shelter.

Not just New York was hurt. Cities up and down the northeast coast were also paralyzed. In Massachusetts, drifts were reported over 40 feet high. Philadelphia was buried under tons of snow. Even Washington, D.C., was closed down. Trains were stalled in snowdrifts. Boats capsized from high winds in the harbors.

The blizzard raged for 36 hours. The official depth measurement was 20.9 inches, but this did not include the giant drifts. Snowdrifts blocked entrances to buildings and homes. They made movement in the city almost impossible for days.

An ice bridge formed across the East River, joining the borough of Brooklyn with Manhattan. Some people managed to cross the bridge. They slipped and stumbled on the slick ice, just to be able to say, "I walked to Manhattan."

But there was not much sport in the storm. The Blizzard of '88 still stands as the deadliest and most destructive on this continent. Over 200 people died in New York City alone. Farmers outside the city died as they struggled to get their livestock safe into their barns. Hundreds of horses, cows, small animals, and birds froze to death. One farmer froze to death just trying to get from his barn to his house. More than 200 boats were beached or destroyed in the waters along the Eastern Seaboard between Washington, D.C., and Massachusetts.

Activities

Remembering the Facts

Decide whether each of the following statements is true or false. Write **True** or **False** next to each sentence.

1. People had plenty of warning that this enormous storm was approaching.

2. In 1888, New York City was already one of the most crowded cities in the United States.

3. A severe Canadian cold front collided with a tornado.

4. The blizzard began just after people had gotten to work on the morning of March 12.

5. Hurricane-force winds swept down the streets of the city at 84 miles per hour.

6. New York was the only city of the Northeast paralyzed by the blizzard.

7. Some places in Massachusetts reported drifts over 20 feet tall.

8. Boats safely rode out the storm in their harbors.

9. The blinding snow bombarded the city for 36 hours.

10. An ice bridge formed between the island of Manhattan and the borough of Brooklyn.

Understanding the Story

Write a short paragraph explaining what you would do in one of the following situations.

1. What could you do to make sure you did not get lost between your house and your barn in a blinding snowstorm?

2. What would you do to protect yourself from the freezing cold and hurricane-force winds?

Vocabulary

Write a sentence using each of the following words from this story.

- forecast

- predictions

- accurate

- satellites

- radar

- frigid

- tropical

- taper

- stranded

- paralyzed

Towering Inferno

AP/WIDE WORLD PHOTOS

It seemed impossible: No one could fly directly into the Empire State Building. In 1945, the 1250-foot structure was the tallest building in the world. Located in the center of New York City, it towered above all the other skyscrapers. You could see it for miles.

Even so, it happened on a Saturday morning, July 24, 1945. A twin-engine B-25 bomber, which had flown on many successful missions in World War II, slammed head first into the seventy-eighth and seventy-ninth floors of the Empire State Building.

It was supposed to be a routine flight from Bedford, Massachusetts, to Newark, New Jersey. The pilot was Lieutenant Colonel William F. Smith. He was 27 years old, and he had been decorated for two years of combat flying during the Second World War. The only other passengers were Staff Sergeant Christopher Domitrovich and a young sailor who was hitchhiking a free ride home.

By the time they flew over LaGuardia Airport on Long Island, New York, weather conditions were very bad. Fog and drizzle made it nearly impossible to see. The air traffic controller advised Smith to land until conditions improved. But the pilot felt he could surely finish the trip over Manhattan Island to Newark. As

Smith headed out over New York City, the air traffic controller warned him that the clouds were so low he would not be able to see the top of the Empire State Building. Smith didn't see how he could miss seeing the Empire State Building. He replied sarcastically, "Roger. Thank you, Tower."

Hundreds of horrified New Yorkers watched the plane roaring over the city at a very low altitude. It flew at eye level past someone working in the office tower on top of Grand Central Station. Another worker, standing on the observation tower of a building in Rockefeller Center, saw the silver plane flying 100 feet *below* him. The roar of the bomber's engines echoed in the canyon-like streets of Manhattan.

There was an enormous explosion as the plane rammed into the Empire State Building at full speed. It hit between the seventy-eighth and seventy-ninth floors, just a little over 900 feet above ground. A huge rocket of flame shot upward, covering the skyscraper. Smashed building fragments showered down on the ground.

Everyone working on the seventy-ninth floor— most of the employees of the National Catholic Welfare Conference—died instantly. So did the pilot and his two passengers.

One of the engines shot across the flaming floor and fell down an elevator shaft. It fell all the way to the basement of the building, leaving 800 gallons of burning gasoline in its wake.

The other engine, and part of the landing gear, plunged down several floors. Then they shot out the opposite side of the skyscraper and crashed through the roof of another building.

Another piece of wreckage sliced through the cable of an elevator passing the seventy-sixth floor at the time of the crash. The elevator went into a free fall. Its operator plunged 75 floors down to the basement. She broke her back and her legs, but the 20-year-old woman amazingly survived the fall.

Firefighters could only get up to the sixty-seventh floor by elevator. They had to carry all their hoses and equipment up the last twelve sets of stairs to try to put out the raging gas-fueled fires.

It was lucky that the accident happened on a Saturday. Normally 15,000 employees worked in the Empire State Building. Hundreds of other visited the observation deck on the eighty-sixth floor. This Saturday, the fog and drizzle kept most of the tourists at home. Fourteen lives were lost, and another 25 injured, but it could have been much, much worse.

In three months, workers had repaired the giant hole. But there are many today who will never forget the morning the bomber crashed into the Empire State Building.

Activities

Remembering the Facts

Complete the following statements with facts from the story.

1. The Empire State Building was _____ feet tall.

2. The weather on the morning of this fatal flight was
   _____ and _____.

3. _____ was the day of the week the crash
   occurred.

4. The pilot of the plane had done two years of combat
   flying during _____.

5. There were only _____ passengers in the plane.

6. The plane hit between the _____ and
   _____ floors.

7. The air controller at _____ airport
   tried to warn the bomber pilot.

8. Normally, _____ employees work in the Empire State Building.

9. One woman miraculously survived when

_____ went into a free fall.

10. Amazingly, it took only _____ months for workers to repair the gaping hole caused by the crash.

Understanding the Story

Write a short paragraph about one of the following questions.

1. How could you protect yourself in a falling elevator?

2. Why do you think the pilot continued despite the air controller's warning?

Vocabulary

Write a sentence using each of the following words from this story.

- structure

- missions

- routine

- decorated

- hazardous

- sarcastically

- altitude

- echoed

- fragments

- wreckage